LA GRAN MUSICA
CLASSICAL COLLECTION

LINGUAPHONE

CLUB INTERNACIONAL DEL LIBRO

PolyGram

USING THIS BOOK

The book has three sections:
Background information about the composer and his times and about the music and performers on the recording.

A MUSICAL REFERENCE CHART which gives you a quick, at-a-glance path through the music.

The LISTENING GUIDE which takes you through the music in detail, explains what is happening, increases your understanding and heightens your enjoyment of it.

You should read the LISTENING GUIDE at the same time as you listen to the music. Or you may prefer to prepare in advance by reading a few paragraphs at a time before you listen. The numbers given at the beginning of each paragraph correspond to the time given on the counter of your CD player.

When you have listened to the music, you may only need the MUSICAL REFERENCE CHART for future listenings, but the detailed comments in the GUIDE are always there for you to check back on and to remind yourself of any particular points, and to go on increasing your involvement with the music and your enjoyment of it.

The colours on the Chart correspond to the colour coding of the numbers at the beginning of each paragraph in the GUIDE; in this way you will easily be able to refer from one to the other.

The moment when the music begins we number 00.00 on the CHART and in the GUIDE, but some CD players begin to count a few seconds before that. Remember this in case the timing on your counter appears to be slightly out of synch with our text.

LA GRAN MUSICA
CLASSICAL COLLECTION

VANTONIO VIVALDI

(1678-1741)

Deutsche
Grammophon

Linguaphone Institute Limited
St Giles House
50 Poland Street
London W1V 4AX

© 1994 Polygram International Ltd and
CIL, Sociedad Anónima de Promoción y Ediciones

English translation of *Chart* and *Guide* © 1995 Linguaphone Institute
Limited

Printed and bound in Spain by
G. ENAR, S.A.
ISBN: 84-599-3444-6 (o.c.)
ISBN: 84-599-3445-4

THE COMPOSER

Antonio Vivaldi, whose father was a baker before he became a violinist and opera impresario, has been accused by detractors of turning out pieces of music the way a baker turns out loaves of bread. And yet Vivaldi offered, and offers, a great deal more than quantity. The twelve concertos comprising his collection *L'Estro Armonico (The Spirit of Harmony)*, were "the most influential music publication of the first half of the 18th century" in the words of his biographer, Michael Talbot. Bach, seven years Vivaldi's junior, transcribed some of them and was eager for more, and the composer and theorist, Quantz, used Vivaldi's concerto form as an example of how such pieces ought to be composed. Born in Venice on 4 March, 1678, Vivaldi was a sickly child who suffered from asthma or possibly heart disease. He studied music while training for the priesthood. In 1703 he was ordained, and in the same year he became *maestro di violino* at the Ospedale della Pietà, a church-run orphanage and school for indigent girls. in 1716 he became the institution's *maestro de' concerti*. By then, his fame as a violin virtuoso and as a composer was international, and in 1718 he began a series of tours that took him and his court-like entourage through much of Italy (where he was known as 'the red priest', because of the colour of his hair) and as far afield as Vienna and possibly Prague. In addition to hundreds of instrumental concertos and sonatas, he wrote a great deal of liturgical music and dozens of operas, and he himself became an opera impresario. Anna Girò, one of his pupils from the orphanage, made a name for herself as an opera singer in the mid-1720s, when she was in her mid-teens. From then until the end of Vivaldi's life, she and her sister travelled with the composer and were commonly believed to be his mistresses, although he denied the rumour. In middle age Vivaldi was a wealthy man, but lavish living and a decline in his popularity gradually reduced him to poverty. When he died, on 28 (or 27) July 1741, during a visit to Vienna, he had to be given a pauper's burial. Within a few decades of his death, his music had virtually been forgotten, but since the 1920s his prestige and popularity have steadily revived.

THE WORKS

In or around 1725, Vivaldi published *Le Quattro Stagioni (The Four Seasons)* - the first four of a set of twelve concertos collectively entitled *Il cimento dell'armonia e dell'inventione* (The Contest Between Harmony [Reason] and Invention [Imagination]). But in writing the dedication, to the Bohemian Count Wenzeslaus von Morzin, he mentioned that the pieces had been composed and performed some years earlier. Each three-movement concerto is scored for string orchestra with solo violin, and each is preceded by a 'descriptive sonnet' and contains onomatopoeic cues, such as the 'singing of birds' and 'the barking dog' (*Spring*); 'the

Portrait of Antonio Vivaldi. Museum of Music Bibliography, Bologna.

cuckoo', 'different kinds of winds' and 'the young peasant's lament' (*Summer*); 'the drunkard' and 'the animal fleeing' (*Autumn*); and 'chattering teeth' and 'the sirocco wind' (*Winter*). Musical imitations of nature were common in Vivaldi's day, but in our day his *Four Seasons* has become the most famous example of the practice - and indeed, one of the most delightful and best-loved examples of Baroque instrumental music as a whole. Of the other works heard here, the two concertos, like many others by Vivaldi, illustrate a particular mood or idea - 'L'amoroso' (The Lover), with solo violin and the folk-tinted Concerto 'alla rustica', which has no solo instrument. The intense Sinfonia 'Al Santo Sepolcro' was probably written for the Pietà.

5

18th century print of Vienna, a city visited by Vivaldi on his concert tours.

THE POLITICAL BACKGROUND

Although Venice was rich in cultural activity in Vivaldi's day, as a political entity the once-glorious Venetian Republic was in its death throes, maintaining its independence by practising strict neutrality towards Austria, Turkey and other major powers. Like other artist-craftsmen of his day, Vivaldi survived by kowtowing to the potentates, petty and otherwise, of a variety of kingdoms, principalities, dukedoms and ecclesiastical territories in Italy and Central Europe.

.THE CULTURAL SCENE

Besides Vivaldi, composers active in the 1720s - an extraordinarily rich period for European music - included Bach, Handel, Alessandro and Domenico Scarlatti, François Couperin, Rameau, Dandrieu, Clérambault and Marcello. John Gay's *The Beggar's Opera* was first heard in 1728. Montesquieu's *Persian Letters*, Voltaire's *Henriade*, Defoe's *Moll Flanders* and Swift's *Gulliver's Travels* were published during that decade. The painters Watteau, Boucher, Piazzetta, Canaletto, Tiepolo and Hogarth were all active.

Venetian Ambassador 18th century.

> 1724: *Gin drinking becomes widespread in England*
> 1727: *Coffee first planted in Brazil*

THIS RECORDING'S CONDUCTOR

HERBERT VON KARAJAN, who was born in Salzburg in 1908 and died in Anif, near Salzburg, in 1989, was one of the most successful and widely admired performing musicians of the second half of the 20th century. Through live appearances and recording with many of the world's greatest orchestras and opera ensembles, and especially with the Berlin Philharmonic - of which he was principal conductor from 1955 to the end of his life, and which he conducts in these recordings - he influenced fellow musicians and public taste for two generations.

INSTRUMENTS:

1 Violin I 3 Viola 5 Double Bass
2 Violin II 4 Cello

'The Four Seasons"

SPRING — 11'16"

ALLEGRO					LARGO		ALLEGRO	
AWAKENING SPRING	SINGING BIRDS	MURMURING SPRINGS	STORM	SINGING BIRDS	RUSTLING LEAVES, BARKING DOG, SLEEPING PEASANT	THEME REPEATED	COUNTRY DANCE	THEME REPEATED
00:00	00:32	01:12	01:43	02:20	00:00	01:27	00:00	02:43

SUMMER — 10'50"

ALLEGRO NON MOLTO							ADAGIO			PRESTO	
TIREDNESS	CUCKOO	TURTLE DOVE	GOLDFINCH	BREEZES	WINDS	LAMENT	FLIES/BLOWFLIES	FLIES	BLOWFLIES	STORM	SOLO
00:00	01:15	02:10	02:38	02:50	03:05	03:46	00:00	00:45	01:34	00:00	00:48

"L'amoroso"

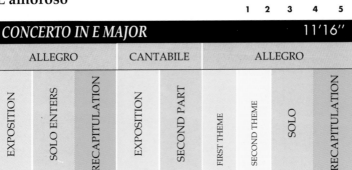

CONCERTO IN E MAJOR — 11'16"

ALLEGRO			CANTABILE		ALLEGRO			
EXPOSITION	SOLO ENTERS	RECAPITULATION	EXPOSITION	SECOND PART	FIRST THEME	SECOND THEME	SOLO	RECAPITULATION
00:00	00:44	03:28	00:00	01:15	00:00	00:12	00:30	03:37

"Al Santo 9

SYMPHON

ADAGIO M	
EXPOSITION	CHORAL
00:00	01:21

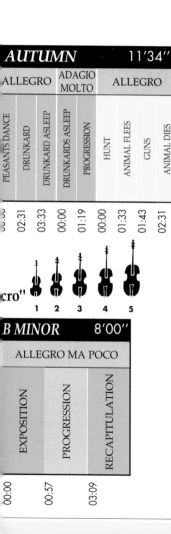

AUTUMN — 11'34"

ALLEGRO			ADAGIO MOLTO		ALLEGRO			
PEASANTS DANCE	DRUNKARD	DRUNKARD ASLEEP	DRUNKARDS ASLEEP	PROGRESSION	HUNT	ANIMAL FLEES	GUNS	ANIMAL DIES
00:00	02:31	03:33	00:00	01:19	00:00	01:33	01:43	02:31

WINTER — 9'00"

ALLEGRO NON MOLTO					LARGO			ALLEGRO					
COLD	STORM	RUN & STAMP	WINDS	CHATTERING TEETH	RAIN	SOLO	CADENCE	WALK ON ICE	CAREFUL WALK	FALLING DOWN	RUNNING	SIROCCO	NORTH WIND
00:00	00:34	01:07	01:19	02:26	00:00	00:58	01:47	00:00	00:33	00:43	00:55	01:53	02:32

B MINOR — 8'00"

ALLEGRO MA POCO		
EXPOSITION	PROGRESSION	RECAPITULATION
00:00	00:57	03:09

"Alla Rustica"

CONCERTO IN G MAJOR — 5'05"

PRESTO		ADAGIO		ALLEGRO		
EXPOSITION	DEVELOPMENT	EXPOSITION	CADENCE	EXPOSITION	DEVELOPMENT	RECAPITULATION
00:00	00:33	00:00	01:18	00:00	00:47:	01:40

THE FOUR SEASONS

INSTRUMENTS:

Soloist: Violin.

Orchestra: Violin I, Violin II, Viola, Cello and Double Bass.

The evocation of nature through music has been one of the basic aims of many composers through the ages. Various means have been used to achieve this, but the most favoured one has been based on instruments imitating the sounds of nature, such as birdsong, the sound of the wind and other atmospheric phenomena, the simple songs of the people at country gatherings, etc. Vivaldi wrote these four concertos for violin and string orchestra, designing each one to represent a particular season of the year and producing one of his most descriptive and popular works. He portrays the natural atmosphere of each season using all the means in his power. The result is for us to enjoy.

SPRING OP. 8 Nº 1 CONCERTO IN E MAJOR RV269 (11' 16)

1. ALLEGRO (3'27)

THE AWAKENING OF SPRING

00:00 This first concerto begins with a joyful melody in E major (a bright key*) played by the violins, which vividly evokes the jubilant mood at the birth of spring. The gradual increase in intensity in this first fragment describes the birth of a nature brimming with life, where the atmosphere is flooded with light and colour.

00:08 The first phrase is repeated, this time with less intensity - *piano* (softly), a common technique in the composition of Baroque music.

00:16 A melodic fragment appears, with the intensity of the beginning - *forte* (loud). Vivaldi will use this fragment as a bridge to join the different appearances of the solo violin; that is, as a kind of refrain* which suggests the rustic joy of spring.

00:24 This same piece is repeated *piano*.

THE SINGING OF BIRDS

00:32 The principal violin begins, followed by the soloist from the second violins, and then by the soloist from the first violins, each one imitating with its own sound the singing of three different birds. The perfection in the descriptive powers of this work is a milestone in the history of music.

01:04 The orchestra presents the main theme* again as a refrain.

*KEY: a system of music in a scale of notes related to each other, based on a particular note. As with colours, music has different shades; arranging E major suggesting bright, C minor dark, etc.

*REFRAIN: part of the composition that recurs, such as a chorus.

*THEME: A musical idea, generally melodic, capable of being developed or varied.

THE MURMURING OF SPRINGS

01:12 Now the violins play phrases based on short intervals*, and this imitates the soft murmur of water.

01:27 A modulating bridge* leads us towards a recapitulation of the refrain, this time in a different key.

THE STORM

01:43 The full orchestra plays groups of rapid notes, the violins play two ascending scales* and the orchestra then returns with a modulation which introduces the solo violin. Vivaldi describes in a masterly way the imminent arrival of the storm, and at every moment he recreates the violent atmosphere of spring.

01:50 The soloist alternates with the orchestra, playing arpeggios* at great speed, while the orchestra repeats the theme with rapid notes.

02:12 The orchestra plays the refrain again and this serves as a bridge to introduce the next appearance of the soloist.

THE SINGING OF BIRDS

02:20 The soloist imitates the singing of the birds again, supported by the soloists of the first and second violins. This time the solo appearances vary, creating a multitude of tones and different sound effects, fulfilling the composer's ideas for evoking spring.

02:37 A phrase extracted from the melody* which opened the concerto is presented by the orchestra as a refrain.

02:49 The soloist plays a final sequence in a song-like way before finishing the movement.

*INTERVAL: the distance in pitch between any two sounds.

*MODULATING BRIDGE: a musical fragment which joins two themes in different keys.

*SCALE: an ascending or descending succession of adjoining notes.

*ARPEGGIO: the notes of a chord played in succession.

*MELODY: the linear arrangement of notes and intervals more commonly known as a tune.

Antonio
Visentini:
'The Concert at
the Villa',
fragment.

03:02 The full orchestra repeats the refrain twice, the first time *forte*, the second *piano*, to finish the piece. So ends the explosion of joy at the arrival of the season of flowers and colour. Vivaldi has achieved a masterly control of descriptive musical effects.

2. LARGO E PIANISSIMO SEMPRE (3'21)

00:00 Vivaldi now describes three basic elements of the tranquillity of spring. The three appear superimposed in a brilliant contrapuntal* manner where the violins sustain a kind of harmonic support by means of brief appearances made of small intervals, signifying the rustling of leaves and plants. The violas keep up the rhythm imitating the barking of a dog. The solo violin begins with the fragment of a melody in the style of an arpeggio, which describes the calm and somnolent atmosphere of the scene where the shepherd is asleep.

*CONTRAPUNTAL: having the characteristics of COUNTERPOINT.

*COUNTERPOINT: The relationship between two or more independent melodic lines when they are combined.

*CADENCE: final section of a musical phrase used to indicate the end of it.

00:34 We now hear a second phrase from the soloist based on a succession of chords finishing with a cadence* that leads us to the repetition of the melody.

01:27 Repetition of the theme with slight variations in the melody.

01:54 Second fragment with variations in the same way.

02:44 Final fragment played as a cadence.

03:04 With the accompaniment of violins and violas evoking the rustle of leaves and plants and the barking of a dog, this second movement finishes in the midst of the calm and tranquillity of a spring afternoon in the country.

3. ALLEGRO (4'28)

COUNTRY DANCE

00:00 The third movement begins with a very dance-like melody played by the violins accompanied by the violas, cellos and basses on a pedal* point. This imitates the droning* sound of some instruments used in folk music such as bagpipes and panpipes.

00:09 The same phrase is repeated, this time more softly (*piano*).

00:17 Again, with the same intensity as at the beginning, the violin plays a second part of the melody.

00:23 The violins introduce a third melodic motif*.

00:34 The solo violin enters accompanied only by the continuo* and plays a melody deeply imbued with the rustic spirit.

01:00 The principal theme of the dance, in E major, is taken over by the orchestra but now in a minor* key. The contrast between the two phrases shows us how the same melody played in different keys (major or minor) will produce different impressions on the listener.

01:08 A progression of chords* which is then repeated *piano* leads us to a new theme.

*PEDAL: sustained note or notes in a supporting role, usually underneath the melody.

*DRONE: sustained bass notes, reminiscent of the sound of bagpipes.

*MOTIF: a short, recognisable melodic or rhythmic idea. Several may contribute to a theme.

*CONTINUO: the combination of a single bass line (usually cello) and chords played by a keyboard instrument.

*MINOR KEY: one of the two predominant musical scales containing the interval of a minor third from its key note. A major key uses the major third.

*CHORD: three or more notes played at the same time.

01:19 The theme which we have just heard is made up of the alternation of melodies in triplets* between the violins, the violas, the cellos and the basses.

01:37 The solo violin comes in again playing scales and arpeggios, modulating towards a choral type of passage played by the orchestra. The pastoral mood is momentarily changed.

02:17 The violins repeat small rhythmic figures, the harmonies of which progress towards a recapitulation of the main theme.

02:43 The orchestra plays the main theme and then repeats it in a minor key, adding new harmonic richness portraying the joy of the people.

03:21 The violin plays a solo in a cadenza* style accompanied only by the cello and the double bass playing a pedal note imitating the drone.

03:51 Recapitulation of the main theme, surrounding us again with the pastoral atmosphere which has dominated the whole concerto and which is finished with a cadence.

SUMMER OP. Nº 2 CONCERTO IN G MINOR RV 315 (10'50)

4. ALLEGRO NON MOLTO (5'48)

TIRED FROM THE HEAT

00:00 Vivaldi expresses the effect summer heat has on us with a theme based on short motifs which mimic slow, deep breathing, played by the orchestra with well-spaced silences.

*TRIPLET: three notes of equal value played in the time of two.

*CADENZA: a part of the concerto where the soloist demonstrates technical gifts and inventiveness.

00:28 Now the violins play descending scales which are continued by the violas, cellos and basses and repeated a tone higher, evoking a quiet, relaxed atmosphere.

00:50 We hear the motif again, three ascending notes separated by silences.

THE CUCKOO

01:15 The solo violin comes in with a long phrase based on very quick notes which, with the help of the continuo, imitates the call of the cuckoo.

01:47 The full orchestra takes up again the motif of the solo violin, expanding it and playing it with appropriate feeling.

01:53 The same theme from the beginning reappears as a refrain to introduce the solo violin imitating a new bird.

THE TURTLE DOVE

02:10 While the double bass plays a pedal note with slight variations that remind us of the cuckoo we have just heard, the solo violin plays a phrase based on alternating small intervals and octave* leaps. The phrase ends with three short ascending scales. The orchestra plays this last motif with a bridge to reintroduce the solo violin.

THE GOLDFINCH

02:38 Now the solo violin, unaccompanied, plays a phrase based around trills* in a high register, to imitate the song of the goldfinch.

*OCTAVE: interval between two notes of the same name, ie 8 notes.

*TRILL: alternation of two adjacent notes, often played quickly. Used to ornament a melody.

16

C.A. Guardi (1698-1760): 'The Nuns' Parlour'.

SOFT BREEZES

02:50 The same theme that the orchestra played before as a bridge passage is now developed, but the atmosphere becomes progressively more restless, alternating the two degrees of intensity, *piano** and *pianissimo** evoking the slow sighing of a breeze.

DIFFERENT KINDS OF WIND

03:05 The orchestra describes in an agitated movement the force of the wind - the north wind - in ascending and descending progressions.

03:33 The theme from the beginning of this movement reappears as a refrain, and this introduces the final part.

*PIANO: softly.

*PIANISSIMO: very softly.

03:46 The soloist performs a phrase of smooth notes in a descending harmonic progression*, accompanied only by the continuo playing the first beat of each bar. In this melody a young peasant is lamenting his uncertain fate. A cadence from the solo violin introduces the last section of the movement with full orchestra.

05:14 Wide intervals are played by the violins in quick figures, accompanied by the violas and the cellos, repeating the same note in every bar, and the increasingly agitated atmosphere is expressed in a clearly Italian style.

05:25 Ascending and descending scales played by the violins bring us to the final cadence played by the whole orchestra. They play brief motifs based on descending melodic progressions* that change the previous sadness into joy.

5. ADAGIO (2'16)

FLIES AND BLOWFLIES

00:00 The solo violin plays a slow melody with which Vivaldi intends to convey the tranquil atmosphere of a summer rest. The accompaniment is played by the violins with a rhythmic repetition of the notes that make up the harmony.

00:17 The rest is interrupted by the flies and blowflies which are always around in the summer. Violins, violas, cellos and double basses repeat the same note over again with great speed (*allegro*).

00:20 Now we experience again the somnolent atmosphere of the beginning where the violin soloist takes up again the melody that was interrupted.

*HARMONY: superimposition of three or more sounds heard singly or successively. The harmony is the result of the succession of chords and their interrelation.

*HARMONIC PROGRESSION: logical succession of 2 or more chords with all notes moving at the same time.

*MELODIC PROGRESSION: linear progression of notes together with the supporting harmony or chords.

00:45 The flies disturb again the tranquillity of summer.

00:50 The soloist continues with the exposition of his beautiful melody.

01:34 The blowflies reappear as a refrain between the melodic expositions of the solo violin.

01:38 The soloist appears for the last time to finish this brief second movement.

01:57 The double basses imitating the flies also appear for the last time, and the solo violin ends holding onto a long note while the violins play the end of their accompaniment.

6. PRESTO (2'46)

SUMMER STORM

00:00 The charged, stormy weather, marvellously captured by Vivaldi, is played by the full orchestra with very short figures at great speed. A series of continuous pauses separate the different fragments of this dizzying passage.

00:06 The same fragment is repeated now in D .

00:10 This passage is based on descending scales played at great speed by the solo violin and the first and second violins. These scales are played in quick succession to evoke the force of the wind and the violence of the storm.

00:23 Now the direction changes to ascending scales.

00:34 The solo violin is introduced with a harmonic progression, but before it comes in the orchestra repeats the motif with brief ascending scales.

00:48 The solo violin enters playing a phrase which calls for all his virtuoso skills and which perfectly describes the restless mood that dominates this movement. The violin plays arpeggios, extensive scales and, for the first time, plays on two strings (double stopping) to bring in the orchestra.

01:07 The orchestra develops new melodies always taken from the initial melodic material. The atmosphere is continuously restless and full of contrasts.

01:31 The solo violin is now accompanied by the double basses performing a playful rhythmic figure. The background describes the wind that causes the storm.

01:44 The orchestra returns with melodic progressions based on the principal theme, which give the impression of unease.

01:59 The soloist then performs quick arpeggios while playing an ascending scale on the first string.

02:03 The orchestra answers with the same descending scales as before.

02:13 The solo violin returns with very fast arpeggios.

02:18 Now the orchestra plays an ascending scale and then finishes with a descending one.

02:22 The last appearance of the soloist before the end of the concerto.

02:27 The orchestra finishes this restless last movement which ends this concerto devoted to summer.

AUTUMN OP. 8 N° 3 CONCERTO IN F MAJOR RV 293 (11'34)

7. ALLEGRO (5'26)

PEASANTS DANCING AND SINGING

00:00 The orchestra plays a simple, beautiful dance melody, which will serve as a main theme and will appear as a refrain in between the different appearances of the orchestra and the violin.

00:06 The same melody is repeated, but this time an octave lower.

00:13 The orchestra answers, playing a second phrase from the melody.

00:17 The same passage leads now to the recapitulation of the main melody which is repeated this time less strongly (*piano*).

00:28 The solo violin plays on two strings the melody for two voices which imitates the merry, relaxed song of the peasants. The continuo part sketches in the harmonic bass of the dance, which is repeated quietly as an answer.

00:41 A new motif, inspired by the melody, is played and repeated quietly by the soloist. We can appreciate the dancing spirit of this movement during the whole development of the theme.

00:56 The main theme is repeated as a refrain by the full orchestra.

01:06 The first entry of the solo violin playing its own material, based on arpeggios during the first part and descending scales in the second.

01:22 The orchestra returns with the main motif from the theme, giving way all the time to the solo violin who plays scales and arpeggios at great speed.

02:09 The orchestra plays the main theme again, this time in a minor key. This part of the piece continues with a progression leading to a recapitulation of the theme played again in the original major key.

THE DRUNKARD

02:31 Vivaldi uses the solo violin to describe a drunkard, a friend of the young wine which autumn brings us. There are ascending and descending scales and all kinds of embellishments which are performed by the soloist, discreetly accompanied by the continuo part.

03:05 The orchestra returns with the main theme of the dance.

03:11 A new part of the dance is timidly introduced by the orchestra.

03:26 The drunkard appears again, represented by quick scales performed by the solo violin.

THE SLEEPING DRUNKARD

03:33 The first movement of *Autumn* portrays a feeling of calm with a melody made up of long figures played by the soloist that aims to describe the rustic tranquillity of the drunkard asleep.

03:56 The melody which we have just heard is repeated and developed with long notes by the solo violin, accompanied by the orchestra using rhythmic figures to convey the tranquillity and depth of sleep.

04:58 There is now a recapitulation of the main theme with the full orchestra, indicating the end of the first movement. The instrumentation of this passage enables us to visualise the ochres, dark greens, yellows and all the various colours of autumn, all described by

Vivaldi by means of languorous melodies and shy interventions by the orchestra.

8. ADAGIO MOLTO (2'36)

THE SLEEPING DRUNKARDS

`00:00` The whole of this movement is in absolute calm. The violins perform motifs based on descending scales in a choral manner, and the harmony is maintained by the violas, cellos, double bass and continuo, played in the form of an arpeggio. In this tranquil atmosphere we can hear the slow breathing of the sleeping drunkards.

View of Venice in a painting of the 18th century. School of Guardi.

`01:19` A chord from the violins announces that there is going to be a harmonic progression. If we listen carefully to each one of the tones we can imagine the autumnal peace where everybody sleeps off the drunkenness brought on by wine and merry-making.

9. ALLEGRO (3'32)

THE HUNT

00:00 Now we hear an exposition of the main theme - a refrain - of the hunt by the whole orchestra. The rhythm in this movement evokes the hunters going to the hunt at daybreak with their horns and dogs.

00:09 A modulation leads us to the second theme, played by the violins.

00:16 The melody in this second theme reminds us of the melody in the first concerto dedicated to spring. The phrase is played first *forte* and then *piano*.

00:27 The first theme is introduced again by the orchestra in the manner of a refrain.

00:36 Now the solo violin comes in playing for the first time the second theme in two voices (on two strings).

The rhythmic character of 'The Hunt' is maintained throughout.

00:51 The refrain is again played by the orchestra to give way to the soloist who plays another variation.

01:01 In this second appearance the soloist repeats some melodies already played previously, but after a modulation* he begins a passage of great virtuosity where he can display his whole repertoire of skills.

THE ANIMAL FLEEING

01:33 The soloist plays a tune in an ascending melodic progression performed in triplets, representing the animal in flight pursued by the hunters. In this passage the descriptive character of the music reaches one of its most significant points.

GUNS AND DOGS

01:43 We now hear the sound of the guns and the barking of the dogs which are represented by short entries by the strings.

01:46 The soloist attacks again with scales and arpeggios accompanied by the orchestra playing soberly to begin with but soon joining in to imitate the racket of the dogs in full cry.

02:09 Again the soloist plays a melodic progression in ascending and descending triplets to convey the agitated atmosphere of the hunt.

02:23 We hear the refrain again and then the soloist enters with quick melodic figures that convey the pain of the wounded animal shot by the hunters, and finally we hear noise of the dogs in the background.

*MODULATION:
changing from one key
to another.

DEATH OF THE FLEEING ANIMAL

02:31 The soloist enters with dizzy descending scales and the orchestra accompanies him playing the dogs' motif, representing the wounded animal collapsing to die. The soloist returns with discordant notes and after a trill passes onto the second theme. The animal is dead, and so the hunt is over.

03:04 The orchestra plays the second theme leading to the final recapitulation. This last part does not seem to be quite in keeping with the dramatic character of the work, but rather to conform to the rules of composition of the times, to which the composer has to submit.

03:10 Recapitulation of the main theme and end of the concerto.

WINTER OP. 8 N° 4 CONCERTO IN F MINOR RV 297 (9'00)

10. ALLEGRO NON MOLTO (3'29)

SHIVERING IN THE FROZEN SNOW

00:00 The orchestra plays an introduction based on discordant notes to give the impression of snow falling and the cold of winter. This whole movement conveys a freezing atmosphere in contrast with the warm melodies of the other concertos.

A VIOLENT STORM

00:34 The solo violin plays a melody of descending scales and arpeggios that announces the impending snow storm. This is accompanied by the orchestra emphasising the harmony and the rhythm in between the different phrases of the soloist, who continues to imitate the gusts of freezing wind.

Pietro Longhi:
'The Family
Concert'.
Venice.

00:56 The whole orchestra plays a harmonic progression imitating the shivering produced by the cold, and then passes to the main theme.

RUNNING AND STAMPING TO KEEP WARM

01:07 The orchestra plays quick figures evoking trembling and shivering in winter. The phrase consists of two parts. One of them represents running about to keep warm: this is played repeating the same note; and the other represents the stamping of feet. This last motif is repeated four times.

WINDS

01:19 The solo violin enters again with a progression of short notes that symbolise the body shivering in the cold. He is accompanied by the orchestra imitating sudden blasts of wind.

01:58 The orchestra comes back to develop the original theme, this time playing with dissonant harmonies to evoke the icy atmosphere.

02:16 The soloist now plays extensive arpeggios that end with motifs based on short intervals, which fully demonstrate how many effective ways Vivaldi found to convey the impression of cold.

CHATTERING TEETH

02:26 In this passage Vivaldi uses quick figures and intervals to mimic teeth chattering.

02:56 The orchestra recapitulates the main theme adding a coda* to end the first movement of 'Winter', which has captured so well the mood of cold and agitation.

11. LARGO (2'15)

RAIN

00:00 The soloist plays an inspired melody while the violins imitate the sound of rain drops on the roof tops by playing *pizzicato**. We can also hear the pedal note held by the violas while the double basses emphasize the rhythm and the harmony.

00:31 The soloist now plays a second part of the melody.

00:46 A third fragment of the melody appears indicating the end, to give way to the soloist.

* CODA: the last section of a movement.

* PIZZICATO: technique of plucking the strings with the finger to produce short, detached notes.

00:58 The soloist plays a new fragment of the melody based on the first fragment. The accompaniment continues to describe the sound of the rain.

01:12 The second fragment is played with variations.

01:34 The soloist performs a melody taken from the various melodies that have apppeared so far, and this will finish the second movement.

01:47 The final cadence shows us that the rain is stopping and that the second movement is finishing.

12. ALLEGRO (3'16)

WALKING ON THE ICE

00:00 The solo violin plays a melody with the character of a recitative* that, with its unsure rhythm, evokes walking on ice. With only twenty steps on the ice while the bass holds the pedal note, Vivaldi conveys the atmosphere he wants.

00:22 The full orchestra follows the footsteps of the soloist playing a crescendo leading to the next fragment.

WALKING CAUTIOUSLY AND FEARFULLY

00:33 A triplet motif warns us how careful we must be when walking on ice.

FALLING DOWN

00:43 A series of descending scales played by the violins imitates the unforeseen falls always a danger when walking on snow

* RECITATIVE: type of singing which imitates the rhythm and inflection of declaimed, spoken language.

RUNNING AFTER FALLING DOWN

00:55 The performance of the violin now indicates getting up after falling down and starting to run. The speed of the music gradually increases.

01:33 Rhythmic motifs made up of short notes played at the same time by the full orchestra take us to the next passage.

01:43 The soloist plays very fast arpeggios, ending in a descending scale to imitate the breaking and thawing of the ice.

THE SIROCCO WIND

01:53 This is a warm rhythm in contrast with the playful passage which we have just heard, describing the change of atmosphere with the arrival of the sirocco wind and the warm calm it brings.

THE NORTH AND ALL THE OTHER WINDS

02:32 The soloist attacks with great violence a dizzy, fast melody made up of ascending and descending scales and arpeggios which describe the north wind and all the other winds. The orchestra emphasises the harmony.

02:51 The orchestra joins in with the soloist for the final part of the work in a cadence of ascending and descending scales played at great speed, which describe the agitation and whirlwinds of winter. And so this fourth concerto ends, the last of the four concertos known as 'The Four Seasons'.

CONCERTO IN E MAJOR
RV 271 (11'16)

L'AMOROSO

INSTRUMENTS:

Soloist: Violin

Orchestra: Violin I, Violin II, Viola, Cello and Double Bass.

• •

13. ALLEGRO (4'21)

00:00 The exposition of the first part of the Allegro demonstrates various melodic motifs of a deeply romantic nature which the composer links together to form a complete melody until the arrival of the soloist. This melody will become the main theme as well as the refrain between the different entrances of the solo violin. The motifs making up the main theme are easily recognisable as each one of them is introduced independently and, in some cases, repeated *pianissimo* (very softly). In this way Vivaldi introduces all the melodic material that dominates the whole movement.

00:44 The soloist enters and the orchestra continues playing without the usual pause to mark his entry, as is customary in Vivaldi's violin concertos. The discreet accompaniment of the orchestra supports the soloist's performance.

01:12 The orchestra enters again with new melodic material.

01:36 The soloist returns playing melodic progressions which lead to a recapitulation of the theme which began the movement.

02:07 The orchestra continues playing strongly, underlining the main theme, this time played in a brighter key.

02:21 The soloist plays a melodic progression based on motifs from the main theme.

02:40 The orchestra enters briefly to link the phrases of the soloist, emphasising with its accompaniment the harmonic development of this movement.

02:48 The soloist plays an ascending melodic progression and then a descending one, finishing in a cadence before the orchestra comes in again.

03:28 The orchestra plays a recapitulation of the main theme to finish the movement.

14. CANTABILE (2'25)

00:00 The solo violin begins its passage in this movement *cantabile**, that is, in an expressive, song-like style, probably inspired by one of the many melodies that Vivaldi composed for opera and oratorio.

00:32 The violin emphasises the phrase we have just heard by repeating it in exactly the same way.

01:15 A second part of the melody is now presented by the soloist, accompanied by the strings which support harmonically the melodic theme.

01:41 The second part of the melody is repeated in exactly the same way. The second movement finishes with a cadence.

*CANTABILE: 'singable'. In instrumental music it means 'with expression'.

15. ALLEGRO (4'30)

00:00 The orchestra plays the first theme. This is a very jolly theme based on the method of imitation of a motif or main structural cell. That is to say, a motif is repeated in the same way, or with variations, on the same or different instruments.

00:12 Now the second theme is played by the orchestra. This second theme can be regarded as an answer to the first, giving it the conclusive character which every melody needs.

00:30 The soloist comes in with a short cadenza, which is answered by the orchestra with a motif from the first theme.

00:45 Now the soloist begins his exposition with the melodic material which we have already heard.

01:16 The orchestra responds in the form of a refrain, changing the harmonies of the first theme.

01:31 The soloist again plays his theme which is very fresh and lively.

01:59 The refrain of the orchestra is always in the same key that the soloist has finished in.

02:11 And now the soloist again, continuing with an imitative melody and modulating towards different harmonies, followed faithfully by the orchestra.

02:32 The orchestra plays the refrain.

02:44 The soloist, accompanied by continuo alone, expands on the melody, the material of which is derived from the first theme.

03:07 The soloist plays a progression leading to the recapitulation.

03:37 The orchestra repeats the first and second themes taken from the beginning.

04:07 The soloist repeats the cadenza taken from the beginning in the same way, and the orchestra responds to finish the concerto.

Gaspar van Wittel:
View of Venice.
18ᵗʰ century.

SYMPHONY IN B MINOR
RV 169 (8' 00)

AL SANTO SEPOLCRO

INSTRUMENTS:

Orchestra: Violin I, Violin II, Viola, Cello and Double Bass.

- -

16. ADAGIO MOLTO (3'28)

00:00 The custom of starting a symphony with a slow movement can be traced back to French influence whose musical tradition imposed a formal structure, while the Italian tradition that finally predominated, was less formally based on a pattern of *allegro-lento, lento-allegro*. By means of a chord from the strings, and especially if this chord is mildly dissonant, a mysterious, supernatural effect can be achieved. And this is the way Vivaldi chose to give this piece an atmosphere of heightened emotion.

01:21 After a general pause the violins take command, performing a choral passage with violas and double basses creating an atmosphere where ordinary experience is transcended.

02:45 After another pause a cadence leads to the next movement. This work is permeated by the religious spirit which Vivaldi, as a Venetian priest, knew so well and was so capable of expressing.

17. ALLEGRO MA POCO (4'32)

00:00 The mood in this passage, despite the fact that it is in the tempo *allegro ma poco*, is not very different from the mood of the first movement. The different voices are superimposed resolving dissonances* into consonances successively, creating an atmosphere of profound religious feeling.

00:36 A progression based on a motif of the violin's part leads to a cadence that, although giving the impression that the passage is coming to an end, continues building up a labyrinth of harmonies where the voices mingle with each other.

00:57 Now the cellos take over the harmonic progression while the violins weave a pattern full of consonance and dissonance.

01:44 Now comes a section of imitative character continuing the passage.

02:00 In this passage we hear, sketched by Vivaldi with the vitality and certainty of Baroque music, what appears to be an exercise in harmonic equilibrium making use of dissonance and consonance

*DISSONANCE: a combination of sounds, that does not satisfy the ear. The opposite of consonance.

that two hundred years later would appear in the music of Mahler and Bruckner.

02:50 The violins and double basses perform a dialogue using harmonic progressions which are very advanced technically for the time in which they were written.

03:09 The violins now keep playing high pitched notes while the violas and double basses continue the harmonic progression. The themes which have already been expressed during the movement reappear, keeping up the transcendental atmosphere which pervades the whole passage.

CONCERTO IN G MAJOR
RV 151 (5'00)

ALLA RUSTICA

INSTRUMENTS:

Soloist: Violin.

Orchestra: Violin I, Violin II, Viola and Double Bass.

* *

18. PRESTO (1'12)

00:00 A melody based on folk music and dance is introduced and repeated by the orchestra.

00:12 The orchestra introduces a second melody played *presto* (fast) throughout the movement.

00:23 A harmonic progression leads to a short development portraying the atmosphere of the countryside with melodies and dance rhythms derived from folk music. The whole of the concerto is dominated by this rustic atmosphere.

00:33 The melodic material which has been introduced is now developed. The contrasts between *forte* and *piano* are predominant during the whole of the movement.

00:57 With a modulation, the melody changes to another key, giving the impression that a new theme is about to begin. In reality, it is only a cadence and this ends, perhaps rather abruptly, the first movement of the concerto.

19. ADAGIO (1'30)

00:00 The orchestra plays groups of chords forming cadences which carry us from one harmonic region to another. The slow tempo takes us to the heights of Vivaldi's inspiration, who knew the power of music to transmit all kinds of feelings and could use it with masterly effect. This exposition finishes in a cadence giving way to the last cadence.

01:18 A second smooth cadence played by all the instruments ends the second movement.

The Frozen Lagoon, School of Guardi, Venice.

20. ALLEGRO (2'16)

00:00 The Allegro again has a melody inspired by folk music. This melody, performed by the whole orchestra, is repeated *piano* and presented several times in different keys. This was a technique very much in use in Baroque music and offers the contrasts which enable us to appreciate the melodic language in all its depth.

00:24 Recapitulation of the entire melody.

00:47 As if this were a concerto for soloist, the violin soloists now play melodies from the material previously heard.

01:00 The orchestra answers playing the main theme as a refrain.

01:29 The soloists enter again repeating their previous melodies.

01:40 The orchestra plays the complete theme again and the concerto ends. 'Alla Rustica' was clearly inspired by folk music, or taken from the large body of European-Mediterranean songs and dances built up over the centuries which formed an integral part of the musical culture until the beginning of the revolution by the serial composers in the early years of the 20th century.